NEIL CURRY

SHIPS
IN
BOTTLES

ENITHARMON PRESS 1988

First published in 1988
by the Enitharmon Press
40 Rushes Road
Petersfield
Hampshire GU32 3BW

ISBN 1 870612 30 2 (paperback)
ISBN 1 870612 50 7 (hardcover)

The Enitharmon Press acknowledges financial
assistance from Northern Arts and Southern Arts

Set in Monotype 12 point Bembo (270)
by Gloucester Typesetting Services
and printed by
Antony Rowe Limited, Chippenham, Wiltshire

Cover design by Michael Whittaker

For Jenny

CONTENTS

In a Calendar of Saints *11*

Poppy Heads *13*

Gardens *15*

The Maidenhair Tree *17*

River Gods *19*

Hands *20*

Cave Paintings *21*

To the Glass-blowers *22*

Ships in Bottles *23*

Voyages *24*

Juan Fernandez *26*

Lindisfarne *27*

Galapagos *28*

St Kilda *29*

The Plain People *32*

Memorial to the Vicars of Urswick *35*

The Doll's House *37*

The Fall of the House *39*

Summer '84 Cumbria *41*

Walls *42*

Kingfisher *43*

Ravens *44*

A Hawk from a Handsaw *45*

Stonechat *47*

Mute Swans *48*

Five Winter Evenings *49*

Five Spring Mornings *51*

Four Times Four *53*

Over and Around *54*

Parading Among the Peacocks   57

The Creation of Caedmon   *59*
Mr William Somers Will Now Entertain Us   *60*
Anne Hathaway Composes Her 18th Sonnet   *61*
Rembrandt van Rijn   *62*
George Fox Crosses the Bay   *63*
Boileau to his Gardener   *64*
John Wesley Among the Miners   *65*
Let Christopher Rejoice   *66*
Chatterton   *67*
John Clare and the Acts of Enclosure   *68*
Vincent   *69*
Looking for a Tongue   *70*

Between Root and Sky   71

Lichen   *74*
Toadstools   *75*
Pimpernel   *76*
Lords and Ladies   *77*
Heather   *78*
Lily of the Valley   *79*
Hemlock   *80*
Dandelion   *81*
Ivy   *82*
Fungus   *83*
Hawthorn   *84*

Alonso Quixano Encounters the Sea   85

ACKNOWLEDGEMENTS

Some of these poems first appeared in the following publications: *Adam's Dream, Ambit, Between Comets, Critical Quarterly, Country Life, Encounter, Form, Iron, Labrys, Lancaster Literary Festival Poetry, New Statesman, Outposts, PN Review, New Poetry (PEN), PEN Broadsheet, Priapus, Resurgence, Thames Poetry, Temenos, TLS.*

Between Root and Sky first appeared as a Mandeville Press pamphlet.

I

Wondering which of all the saints
Had been assigned to share the hours with me
On this first day of February,
(The snow beginning to thaw outside
As though touched by these jets of flame-blue
Hyacinth burning in the window)
I found not one name but two: Ignatius
Of Antioch, and Saint Brigid.

Arrested, and shipped in fetters
Back to Trajan's Rome, Ignatius,
Intent upon martyrdom, begged
That no one intercede for him. 'I am
God's own grain,' he wrote, pausing
Among his strictures on the Trinity
And Eucharist, 'and will prove good bread
Though ground in the jaws of the arena's beasts.'

But in Kildare there was no lion's tooth,
Just the dandelion: Brigid's flower.
Patron of things new-born, who turned water
Into milk, not wine, hers is the other
Face of the world. And on Candlemas Eve
She comes to us with her lambs, quickening
The year: abbess and triple-goddess;
Bride The Beautiful: the Celtic Muse.

II

With Concordius their first foot, the saints
Go marching through the pages of the year:
Hermits, and founders of great orders,
Contemplatives, and martyrs to the Faith:
Men like Aquinas, most learned of saints
And most saintly of all the learned;
Or that other Thomas, whose turbulent brain
One Richard le Breton splattered
Over the altar-cloth at Canterbury.

Some, looking for nothing from this world,
Were, like Cuthbert, content that it should shrink
To a rock of Lindisfarne, where grey seals
Bobbed up and blinked their nostrils in surprise;
While in Assisi, Francis could not embrace
Or bless enough of it, were it his Lady
Poverty or the leper's hand. Almost blind,
In the Convent garden of San Damian
He sang his Canticle of Brother Sun:

A chorus of witness in which we hear
Pointers to what may, impossibly,
Prove possible: as when in August 1941,
On the Eve of the Feast of the Assumption,
Maximilian Kolbe, Polish priest,
In the starved dark of Cell Block 13
Took upon himself another man's death;
The carbolic acid sluiced through his veins
Winning one more victory for Golgotha.

There is, it seems, no poppy seed so old
That given a drop of water and some warmth
It will not flower again, breaking the dream
Of its opiate sleep to send new fancies
Shimmering along the blood. After twenty
Centuries, when smart industrialists
Moved back into the silver mines at Laurium
To pocket up the banks of spoil heaps,
There was a moment's hesitation

In the dust, then wild and exotic
Poppy buds came powering up – strange sons
And daughters of blooms that Pliny must have known,
And would have seen stamped out in tesserae
Upon the Aventine, and on the portly
Bellies of black amphorae: Ceres' sign;
Shocks of sheer scarlet in a yellow heat
That twined through stooks and burned against the blue:
Manna for the mind beside the body's bread.

But then what was manna? The word was no more
Than a mute echo that tried to give
A miracle a name. All they could tell
Was that it came after the quails had flown in
With the falling of the dusk and settled
Over the Wilderness of Sin: a gift
From an otherwise indifferent night
In answer to their needs, their dream; and now
An image of the fulfilment of a dream.

For dreams are not caught in the dissonant
Thickets of language, nor strung on time's links;
They come to us with all the inseminate
Anarchy of the image, and every mote
Of the past concurrent, so wherever
A poppy head has nodded in the world
Some seed may lie waiting and from the pit of night
Will delight, bewilder or admonish us
With the ambiguous innocence that is its power.

GARDENS

We smiled together
over the precepts in that old herbal,
vowing, as we valued our eyesight,
    never to gather
  the fruit of the peony
    save at dead of night
and thus 'all unseene of the woodpecker',

    noted too that powdered
periwinkle and earthworm, if taken
at mealtimes, does rekindle a wife's
    love for her husband;
  strange that they would tolerate
    such wild beliefs
in days when heretics, not weeds, got burned.

    But what gardeners they were:
what arbours of trellis work; embroidered
intricacies of bright nosegay-knots;
    thrift and lavender-
  scented walks of evergreen;
    what salves and syrops
of simple herbs for health and provender;

    what workers for Eden.
Though few of us today would freely voice
our dreams of unicorns and rosebuds,
    their secret garden
  has alleyways that may yet
    outpace all our thoughts.
What our lives lack is what our hands fashion.

The Mogul emperor,
Babur, blazed and butchered his way across
the steppes of Asia, then called a halt
        while his warriors
    erected walls around one
        cool sequestered spot
where lilacs shaded white shawls of water.

THE MAIDENHAIR TREE

(for Jenny Brown)

It was a tree that neither of us
    had ever seen before,
its trunk lined and grey, its leaves
like little pairs of green webbed feet
    and strangely fleshy;

but what really stopped us as we stepped
    from stained-glass cloistered gloom
into impartial sunlight?
Remembering Thoreau saying
    how monstrous he thought

it was that people cared so little
    about trees, yet so much
for Corinthian columns?
Of the affront of namelessness,
    the one challenge still

capable of overwhelming knowledge,
    in that its secret lies
not in saying but being;
and not the tawdry masquerades
    of reverie, the

fictions and frippery of longing,
    but plainly and truly
what for the beholder *is*:
the embodiment of the one
    moment; for language

however deftly it may be used
  in the flora, will not
explain the susurrations
of dry leaves, and illustration,
  though perfect of line,

shows nothing of the rings' slow stretching
  and splitting, the great thirst
sucking moisture from the black
earth to breathe it out through the green
  veins of its foliage:

but such realities always must
  admit experience,
not just the thing perceived but
the experience likewise of
  the perceiving mind,

so that tree now cannot simply be
  without the cathedral
close we first found it in, and
our shared memories, both of which
  lie beyond telling.

Now when Achilles fought with the river,
  it came for him,
   hurling a welter of waves
  that fumed and foamed against his shield;
it was a god and not to be taken lightly.

Others came more kindly than Scamander:
  Galatea
   divined one running out clear
  from under the rock that had crushed
young Acis: just gorgeous Ovidian nonsense

of course, not something that one need believe.
  Real rivers
   go slopping along bank-high
  with melt-water, or may dwindle
to a midge-infested trickle before winter

returns to unfurl the implicate
  possibilities
   of ice: metamorphoses
  of such fact being safer far
than worlds that might fight back and exact respect.

HANDS

Once, on a dig, I found
half the handle from what must have been
    a good-sized pitcher:
just crude medieval earthenware,
gritty, unglazed and of no value,
    so I was allowed to keep it.

But what really pleased me
was the way it fitted the shape of
    my own hand. Even so
it was some time before I noticed
in the hollowed-out end the clear mark
    of a finger nail, made there

when the clay was still wet,
and then a faint thumbprint just where my
    thumb went; and I knew
that over the dead years I'd joined hands
with the maker, and though not on oath
    this too was an act of witness.

CAVE PAINTINGS

How did the old hands come by this colour
(that glint of copper late autumn shunshine
        gives to dying bracken)
for the flanks of these portly little
    low-slung Chinese horses here?

Ground haematite, ochre, or whatever?
But look how that slight bulge in the rock-face
        has so fleshed a rib-cage
one half-hears the clatter of their black
    (as stamen of tulips) hooves

go galloping off down the passageways.
Turning to watch them though, you're faced with the
        blunt head of a great bull
aurochs, glaring and snorting out of
    the swirling smoke of his mane.

But beyond all this – the charcoal mammoth
and the herds of ibex – comes the painted
        palm-print. A signature?
The simple affirmation of self?
    A greeting? Or ritual?

What does seem clear is that of the claws, teeth,
antlers, horns, talons and tusks of the dark
        he had no fear at all . . .
or so this would have us believe. Our
    simpler wish: not not to be?

The problem is one of how to paint
An empty wineglass in full sunlight
On a windowsill so as to capture

Those complicities of glass and light
Which at times suggest the glass may be
A consummation of the spirit

Of the light, even while it flings
It off in prism; to capture
Not only the essence and the past

But also the potential; not simply
What things are, but the power of what
They might just possibly become:

The quest which, with their retorts and stills,
Their crucibles and limbecks, alchemists
From Paracelsus down to Jonson's Subtle

All set themselves, pitting opposite against
Elemental opposite in that secret war,
And so busily they never noticed

How in Venice, craftsmen in overalls
Were putting earth – through sand and potash –
To a trial by fire, and their gaffer,

As they called him, once that red
Gob of the metal was twirling through his fingers,
Breathed into it of his own human spirit.

You've seen paper when it's burnt
And turned to ash, yet keeps its shape,

How fine it is? Well, the sails
Were like that, and the rigging

Something spiders might have spun:
Royals from fore to mizzen,

Delicacy and precision overall;
But a touch of fury too

Where the painted figure-heads
Fought through the foam.

And their maker?

No salty tar sitting on the quay
With the tops of his sea-boots rolled.

No, he kept bees, grew begonias,
Lived alone, and never complained.

Why then these vessels – bottled wanderers
Bobbing on a sideboard sea?

Uncorked – might a bright sprite pop out
To meet all wishes, or would it

Be some gaunt Ahab – black
From the scorch of hell –

Cursing the storms that howled inside?

VOYAGES

I

of Sir Humphrey Gilbert

Sailing home on the smallest of the frigates
(It frisked and skittered through the waves),
He sat in the stern reading More's *Utopia*,
Knowing of course that it was too late now.

God, it seemed, had held the Spaniards
South of Florida, among lush hibiscus and sweat,
While those ampler lands to the north cried out
For His austere and puissant Church in England.

But what with musicians, mineralogists,
And morris dancers (these for the allurement,
So they claimed, of the savages), it could have been
The Ship of Fools itself he had command of.

No seed of the word was sown in the red-man's maize.
They scythed their greed across the land instead,
For timber and turpentine, silver and fur,
And fought with each other over the finds.

Some deserted; others grew rebellious;
And Gilbert, to appease them, broke sail on the frigate.
'We are as near to heaven by sea as by land,'
He declared, before the great wave struck.

II

of Mr John Newton

Before the great wave struck, and *The Greyhound*
Dropped into its trough, Newton, blasphemer
And free-thinker, grasped that what was needed
Was the mercy of God: a thought that crashed

Into him with the same force as the wave
The ship, but saved them both. Saved them both
To trade again along the Guinea Coast
'As zealous as a Jesuit for souls'.

A 'genteel trade', he called it, in which was made
But scant use of thumbscrew or yoke; no more
Than custom and prudence did suggest. For blacks
No share in his Amazing Grace as yet.

III

of Capt. James Cook

As yet the god Lono was no more than a name
On the lips of the priests, but a converted
Whitby-collier, looking something between
A Dutchman's clog and a coffin, brought Cook,

That man of charts and quadrants,
To blunder about in paradise.
They draped him in a cape of feathers
And fell down at his feet. Later he fell too,

While his marines were re-loading their muskets.
In their grief the priests dismembered him and wept;
Prayed, they said, that he would one day come again,
But that his godless crew might soon go sailing home.

JUAN FERNANDEZ

The seventh son of an old and honest
Shoemaker, Alexander Selkirk had the bones
Of folk-tale in him from the first;

Gloomy, morose and in high dudgeon,
It was he himself chose
To be put ashore on Juan Fernandez,

With firelock and powder,
One hatchet, his bedroll and a kettle;
But history had a mind to maroon him

In an archipelago of footnotes,
And let Crusoe, bigot, parrot-tamer
And inventor of the goat-skin brolly,

Find the famous footprint instead:
How pantos mime the baser motives.
Anyway, we'd seen Selkirk on our own islands,

Eyes like whelks, snivelling and shivering
Among the empty dunes. Hadn't we smelled
The dirt and almost trodden in the diarrhoea?

When Woodes Rogers saw his fires and sailed in
To pick him up, we knew we'd get no stories.
Diseased and gibbering, hadn't he lost the power of speech?

All afternoon a cold east wind
Had parched the sand to a smooth, scraped vellum
That the cursive run of the tide
Would scrawl across, stipple and etch.
Later, when it had all but
Covered Cuddy's Rock, the dark cormorants
Hung out their wings to dry.

From his scriptorium window
Eadfrith had sketched their great beaks and pebbled
Luxury of that beach. Now though,
There was Jerome's Prolegomena
To be penned. 'Novum opus
Facere me cogis ex veteri . . .'
New work out of the old.

For such tasks, tired dexterities
Are never enough; echoes of echoes.
What's called for is that other gift
Which suberts logic with all the
Nonchalance of nuance: a man
Conscious of the silence flooding his mind
And giving shape to it.

Whirlpools of ribboned interlace
He drew, maelstroms of colour: indigo,
Verdigris, orpiment and woad;
Labyrinths and carpets of praise,
Of spirals, eyed-pelta and plait.
Craftsman, peacock and saint, Eadfrith's
Quills fluttered with the Word.

With FitzRoy's twenty-two chronometers
Ticking on their shelves, Darwin, sick again,
Killed time re-reading Lyell's *Geology*,
Or *Paradise Lost* – his favourite poem.

On deck the crew were plump and happy now.
Roast armadillo and ostrich dumplings
Had brought them round Cape Horn, and the *Beagle*,
Under full sail, was tacking for the Line.

But charting that long, sheep's jaw-bone of a coast
Could not assuage the zealot in FitzRoy.
To substantiate the Flood, evidence
For Genesis: that was what he wanted.

When they landed, Antediluvium
Was at every turn, but nowhere Eden:
Not in such heat; not with such contortions
Of cinder and lava; and not with such

Black Imps of Hell as the iguanas
Crawling and slithering about these Blighted
Encantadas – these Enchanted Islands,
Where the chief sound of life was a hiss,

From the snakes, and from the giant tortoises,
The indomitable galapagos themselves,
As they lurched and lumbered their way inland
Following their ancient paths to water.

Yet in all this new weird, it was the beaks
Of brown finches that dismasted FitzRoy,
And sent him on his solitary way
To slash a red equator round his throat.

I

The map the dominie had tacked up
On the schoolroom wall didn't even show
St Kilda, but then only a foreigner
Would have needed one to find his way past Mull
And Skye, out through the Sound of Harris, then on
For fifty empty miles over the
Oily pitch and swell of the grey
North Atlantic.
            Any St Kildans,
Out of sight of land, with bad weather closing,
Knew they'd only to watch the flight-paths
Of the birds: guillemot and gannet would wreck them
On the stacs round Borreray, while puffins
Scuttering back wave-high to Dun
Would prove a safe guide home to Hirta
And the Village Bay.

II

Birds. Or angels even
They must have seemed, the women
Plucking, in a cloud of feathers,
At the haul of fulmar their menfolk

Had themselves plucked off the cliffs
Of Conachair; cragsmen spidering,
Thirty fathoms down, along ledges
Of guano, dependent on sheer faith

In their neighbours and on a horsehair rope.
Claim life those cliffs could, but always would
Sustain it while there were sea-birds
In such thousands to stew or dry;

Even a gannet's neck, turned inside out,
Made a snug boot, and oil from the fulmar
Not only fuelled their lamps, but was a panacea
For no matter what ills or ailments of the island.

III

Ultima Thule it was
Until the Victorians discovered it,
Sending in their missionaries
To pound out the parable

Of the Prodigal Son
To people who hadn't
Anywhere to stray to
And had never seen a pig.

Then steamers came, and summer visitors
With gimcrack charities and new disease,
Tipping the cragsmen with a penny each
To see them capering about on Conachair;

Pennies that the winter ferryman
Would finger from the eyelids of their dead.

IV

By lantern-light
They loaded a few more
Sticks of furniture
And the last of the sheep,
And then they drowned their dogs.

In the morning,
According to custom,
In every empty house
There was a Bible left
Open at Exodus.

THE PLAIN PEOPLE

I

About a mile off Highway 7
down the road to Conestoga,
the land becomes good:
good, fertile land,
where the earth
would almost stain your fingers;
black earth it is, and with a sheen
to match that on the thick
coats of the horses, that come now
walking warily from winter barns
out onto the fresh fields;
for these are Mennonite fields,
and at the ends of lanes
their mail boxes – one half expects
Black Letter – preach out the names:
Amos Eby, Menno Martin,
Noah Hoyt and all the host
of Brubacher that came
from Pennsylvania in the wagons
a hundred years ago
to buy a mortgaged wilderness,
and stay 'unspotted from the world'.

II

For the Mennonites
the world was once the Netherlands,
till God's own vigilantes
beat, broke and beheaded them;
was Germany, till they were burned
for accursed Anabaptists,
their womenfolk buried alive –

witness Fräulein von Hove's friends
stamping on the ground above her head
to help her die. But the New World
ends the obligation for martyrdom.

III

Pacifists, where peace now
has become anachronistic,
they struggle to preserve
some placid image of their past:
in broad-brimmed hats
and plain black clothes
they drive their buggies
through the lines of Pontiacs;
in their church a literal Bible
and a literal washing of feet.

IV

Drab, yet conspicuous
as a circus,
they tend their stalls
in Kitchener market,
stamping their feet
against the early morning cold –
the dollar is difficult to avoid –
offering up fruit and cookies,
embroidered pinafores, and jars
of Mother Martin's Apple Butter
'made from a recipe
five generations old'.

V

Five generations of shadows,
shadows of martyrs and travellers,
shadows of farmers
and hewers of trees,
they have inherited the names,
and inherited the clothes,
but with them have put on
a terrible purposeless peace,
and all-embracing denial.
Inbred to the point of idiocy
and seeming to glory in it,
they hold their high-stepping horses
on a mean rein.

(*for Brian Dawson*)

I don't know if Matthias Forrest
Would have been taken greatly by surprise
When the news broke in Furness that his parishioners
Had sprung from apes. 'Liars, drunkards, thieves,
And whoremasters following their filthy pleasures',
That was how George Fox had seen them;
And one of his own brothers in Christ had been disgraced:
'Scandalous in his life and negligent in his calling.'

Fragments of the parish history
Survive to flesh out the names on the plaque
That Thomas Postlethwaite had put up in the chancel;
Telling us that one February
John Addison roasted a whole ox on the ice
When the Tarn had frozen over;
And that it was William Ashburner who arranged
And officiated at the cock-fights on Shrove Tuesday.

Great events of course can be worked out
From the dates: that the first awful reading
From King James's Bible would have been William Lindowe's,
And that it was Nicholas Marshall
Who walked in with the Book of Common Prayer, and then
Had to hold out against Cromwell.
And back, through the collapse of the monastery,
Their names go, till that last, first one, Daniel le Fleming,

Who'd have needed a smooth Norman tongue
To lick the North into holy order.
But the wonder of it all is how few of them
There were. Call them together again
And what a flimsy congregation they would seem:
Three pews would seat them all. And yet,
With time spread out like these low fells, one name's no more
Than that sudden twist in the tumbling flight of a plover.

THE DOLL'S HOUSE

Open the doors
and let your little fat pinkies
prowl through these rooms.

There is no cellar
with dark stairs
to frighten the children.

It is a house
with no roots at all.
Come into the hall

and tap the barometer
that hangs on the wall.
It will neither rise nor fall.

In the kitchen
you will touch
the little red paper fire

that glows in the range,
then put your finger
to your mouth

and make a show
of being burned.
They all do.

And you may,
if you will,
mumble my wooden food.

Upstairs, in the bedroom,
you will not fail
to lift up the pretty valance

and find
to your feigned
and loud delight

that there is indeed
a guzunder there.
For this is an old house

and as its ways
are not your ways,
improprieties

are of no account.
But when you find me
and try to lift me,

as I know you will,
you will find
that someone –

oh, it was years ago –
thought fit to stitch me
into my chair.

THE FALL OF THE HOUSE

(for Victoria)

The path up from the lane's so choked
With willow-herb it's hard to tell
How long it's been since someone last
Pulled this door to and heard its tongue
Sneck into the lock behind them.
But with root and scrub already
Slyly stealing in to claim back
Their clearing, all links seem broken.

Yet though the ritual pieties
Of violation have, of course,
Been carried out with boot and brick,
Beer can and bottle, an echo
Persists, still whispering 'family',
As though one of the household gods
Had got himself so settled there
He'd found it hard to move away.

But woods are no place for pity:
Just let one slate shift on the roof
And there'll be such slime down the walls,
Such fat pus of rot in the beams
They'll soon not have the pith to take
Even the weight of a hunting owl
Screeching down death into the rats
That are chewing away the floors.

Some thing implacable, you feel,
Has begun its course: a few planks
May find their way into a fence,
A strand of hair into a nest,
But mite and louse will come and go
Until the day a sudden blaze
Of lupin in a thicket takes
Some walker unawares.

Drought. And all these fells so dry the firs
Could have come shuffling down through the dust
Like long-legged beasts to drink at their pools.

We drank up Mardale. Day after day
A bleached rim yawned wider round its shores.
And then the walls showed: old vertebrae

Breaking through the waters; stones, then roads,
Gaunt rubble of ground-plans. On this side
Holy Trinity, there the Dun Bull.

Finally there was a bridge, hump-backed
Over nothing and going nowhere.
We prayed for the rains to fall and drown that.

WALLS

Not Flaubert, no, not James himself
Could pen a line with syntax packed as tight

As the throughs in these walls written over the fells;
As these walls dancing their grave morris over the fells;

As the grey groynes checking the green surge
Of these fells; as these walls, packed

Shoulder-high for less than threepence a yard.

KINGFISHER

If Christ our king could
In the ammoniac stench of the stable
Suffer at His Nativity to be
Neighbour to slow-breathing beasts,

Then small wonder that the king-
fisher's spark should be struck
In a damp underworld of willow root and worm
Where vole and water-rat splash,

For once the shells split and sapphire
And fire-opal fledge in their filth
And six or seven small spurts of flame
Are tumbled out into the dazzle,

Then earth, air, fire and water meet
In a perfection of balance, trafficking,
Like prayer, between this world and that.
And isn't it then that their mother's

Fabled and other self is said to brood
On a nest of bones, calming the waters,
And granting us glimpses of Eden
In those Mary-blue halcyon days?

RAVENS

Ambivalent boggard
Of the battlefield
Popping open the eyeballs
Of the warm dead

With your great beak,
Once you deserted Noah
And went off to glut yourself
On an abundance

Of floating, bloated bodies,
Yet later were in high feather
Flying in supplies to Elijah
Ravenous in the desert.

Was it as black messengers
On one-eyed Odin's shoulders
That you learned such god-like
Unpredictability,

Stormbirds of doom and deluge
Who have kept London safe
Ever since Bran's head
Was buried on Tower Hill?

'I am but mad north-north-west. When the wind is southerly, I know a hawk from a handsaw.' Hamlet

But when all the cocks
On the steeple tops
Swung their beaks southerly
He knew it for a hernshaw;

And knew himself
For one too: a thin grey
Stick in the mud:
A hunched hieroglyph

Scratched out against the wind.
Patience is it, or perversity
(Cowardice, Artois said)
To stand so, waiting, waiting

For a fat fish to come to you?
But to shift –
So much as a foot –
Could be to betray oneself

And to stir up such mud
As would loose all possible prey;
Even (hunching himself lower)
To catch the awful eye

Of the hunters hawking the high
Streams of the air, bringing them
Hammering down through one's skull.
Yes, to move at all

Could be to become
A handful of feathers
And a dried foot
Kept in a creel for luck.

STONECHAT

tchek   tchek   tchek

Grey stone, boulder and scree
and below the scree
one spire of gorse
a stonechat tops

eyeing the axemen
as they pick out
tuff from slate
to chip and shape;

they in skins,
he, pert braggart,
in a black cap
and new shirt;

eggs in the nest
crack
and the chicks
scrabble and gape.

Summer
follows on summer,
gorse pods pop
in the heat

and the men
of Langdale
knowing the bird
for what it is

listen
and name it,
and name this:
Pike o' Stickle.

MUTE SWANS

Why did Ben Jonson
      like a great battle fleet
Call Shakespeare
      line astern they come
A swan?
      down the river,
And of Avon too
      breaking the water
When he spent the whole of his working life
      with their silence,
By the Thames?
      and such power
He must have seen him
      in a bird,
At Stratford, I suppose,
      the great paddles of their feet
When he'd downed his quill
      working away under the surface,
And wondered at such silence
      these mute swans

I

After the
half-light,
dark is
emphatic
and actual.

II

The metal sun has gone;
a strip of brass
along the world's lead,
as the frost comes,
nickel-plating every blade
of the black grass.

III

Stars of a
pizzicato brilliance
echo the frost:
white beads bouncing
onto cold marble.

IV

The going of the light
does not change
the colours of the water;
they are always
exactly
how we do not see them:
the colours of their sound.

V

Supported on columns
of green light,
the houses
on the harbour
step
into the sea.

I

A photograph
in a darkroom dish:
grey dawn
imprints the world
slowly.

II

Faint craquelure
in the gloss
of dark,
then rich
blue mackerel.

III

A movement
from the half-forgotten
into the unexpected:
drifts of crocus
and a celandine.

IV

A new green
mists over
the black fields
as warm breath does
a mirror.

V

A hawfinch
in a hawthorn
could shock us all
into sudden
leaf.

FOUR TIMES FOUR

I

The coincidence of spring
and dawn: but was that
a child watching the fires
to the east,

II

or a young girl
in the full noon of summer,
turning her face
to feel the southern breeze?

III

With the children asleep now,
her ears caught the sound
of water running westward
one autumn evening.

IV

She felt her age
crossing the cold yard in the dark;
thought she could smell snow
on the hills to the north.

and in the mud
on the bed of a river
there was a stone
that the waters ran
over and around

until a branch came down
and caught
against that stone
and was held
so that the waters fluttered

leaves on its surface
slowed and stayed
drifting and silting
between the forks
of that branch

then small twigs
and clutters of weed
that put down roots
and flowered there

and a water hen
came bringing reeds
and built its nest
and fed its young
among the flowers there

but it left
before the rains came
over the fells
and the level rose
and the branch moved

and in the mud
on the bed of a river
there was a stone
that the waters ran
over and around

Parading Among the Peacocks

The open fires flung giant shadows
Onto the walls behind them: great black monks
Louring over the kindly, venerable men
Who sang and passed the harp
One man to the next down the long table.

The shadows were only shadows, but Caedmon,
Shivering under their menace, knew
That the strings were closing to torture him
And scrambled out into the safety of starlight
To stand a moment, leaning his back

Against the abbey door before stepping carefully
Over the icy cobbles to his bed in the stable,
Where the beasts that night were grumbling
Softly at their trough, and the song waiting
Inexorably for His new singer.

He was not to be found parading among the peacocks
In damask paltock with the slashed puff sleeves
At pageant, tournament or palme-play court.

With ostentation and extravagance the mode,
What kudos was there in a cap and bells
When frieze and fustian were what caught the eye?

Will Somers' colours stayed essentially rhetorical:
Salt after the banquet, that was his style.
He taunted his tyrant with saws about syphilis,

Quibbled for some block to the axeman's rise
And behaved like a harpy at their Mardi Gras,
Having so much to say about wedlock and vows.

Your malcontents often get lured by the cabaret,
Then once let them feel that they're a part of the show
And it's all lickspittle stooge and impresario.

I wonder what I ought to do today.
This autumn weather's still so temperate
You'd almost think that it was early Maie
And that we'd somehow muddled up the date.
I've polish'd all the silver till it shines;
Some bits were tarnish'd, all their sheen quite dimm'd.
I'd like some help, but Will always declines,
Says, 'Cant' you see the hedge is still untrimm'd?'
I really think our love's begun to fade.
He nags me so. 'The milliner thou ow'st,'
He says, 'and did we need that new lampshade?
It's not on trees you know that money grow'st.'
    And then he's off to London with 'I'll see
    You, chuck. Now don't you fret. I'll write to thee!'

REMBRANDT VAN RIJN

In Amsterdam our sometime Anabaptist
Acts out Bacchus now, with a great tall glass,
And Saskia, disapproving, on his lap.

He has reached twenty-nine and found success,
But telling years observe those changing hats
And how the muscles round his mouth relax

As failure, deaths and debt score up their tally
On his face, and the new rôle is Saint Paul.
For these are not soliloquies in paint,

Not private puddlings in the pus of sorrow;
The sitter is the motley in the mirror
While Rembrandt studies to perform van Rijn.

On the beach at Bardsea, the cocklewomen
Stood watching, waiting, dry-eyed for them to drown.
Around their horses' hooves a rip-tide was racing
And swirling away the brogs of gorse

That had marked safe-passage over the sands,
So now it was too late even for them to turn.
But that speck against the dark sky,
What was it? Was it a star rising?

Was it a sign? Later they would tell
How the great God Himself had parted
The waters; how that Quaker hat of his,
That stayed, God save us, undoffed

Even at Swarthmoor, had been a halo
Round his head; would bear witness
To the grit that lodged in the hard shells
Of their cockled hearts as he rode towering by.

Yew trees shade my lawns, and honeysuckle climbs
The lattice round my windows at Auteuil
Thanks to you, Antoine, my good, green-fingered
And industrous friend. I've watched the careful way
You cultivate my grounds, and only wish
That I could cut the brambles and the thorns
Out of this melancholy and untidy mind of mine,
Could tear my tangled faults out by the root.

But no doubt you think that you're the only one
Who works in this green garden, as you weed the flowers
And prune the trees, and clip the hedge
And roll the lawn, then mend the fence,
And never-ending fetch and carry water
In your buckets to quench the thirsty soil.

Oh but, Antoine, if you had to – *had* to, mark you – write:
A graceful, decorous and polished piece of work
That turned dry thistles into pinks and roses,
Gave elegance and dignity to the gnarled
And commonplace, got right down to the tiniest
Roots of things, and yet was never,
Even for one instant, seen to stoop,
You'd gladly take your shovel in your hands
And level me a hundred acres overnight, I think,
Before you'd try your strength again with words,
With riotous gangs of them wrangling inside your head.

The dirt, dear God, the squalor and the stench
Of those men; why, when one wept I will swear
That teardrop was the first water to touch
His face in weeks, and nothing but liquor
Down his gullet, I should think. And yet he did weep,
Shuddered and twitched too, like a hanged man on the rope,
But the rope that day was the Lord's and hauled
Not at his neck but his immortal soul.

Such was the spectacle: God's great drama:
Unlooked-for grace that grasped a sinner's life
And shook it, as any man might shake a
Stopped clock upon the kitchen mantelshelf
To get it going; then how they chimed out when Charles
Set the rich wafer of his words upon their tongues,
And stole from the Devil those enchanting tunes.
We fished in the ditches, but we brought back pearls.

For although he is to die of drink and debt
    in the King's Bench,
He is dried out now and singing for David.

For whereas the watchmen in St James's Park
    would strike him down with their staffs,
Here at least they let him pray without ceasing.

For although 'Silly fellow! Silly fellow!' they
    call him,
He has a garden with pinks to tend, and in his
    room paper and pens enough for *Jubilate Agno*
    to grow daily.

For although the rat has bit poor Jeoffry's
    throat,
The considerations of this cat will become
    immortal.

For although Nancy and her daughters deserted
    poor Kit,
All the beasts, birds, fish, flowers and gems of
    the world will worship and rejoice with him
    in his own Magnificat.

For whereas God once bent back His bow to smite
    down His enemies,
Christopher has undertaken to re-write His Psalms,
    and is now wearing, like a scarf around him,
    the exultant rainbow of His Love.

The last week in August they'd buried a boy
By Shoe Lane Workhouse in the paupers' pit.
Now Wallis's picture's what people remember:
Young Mr Meredith's lovely imposture:
So elegant and limp in his plum-coloured trousers
And baring his throat to the draught from the window.
One could see St Paul's through the morning mist;
Papers on the floor to give an air of disorder;
That puny plant in flower on the sill.
The picture was varnished and two years later
Meredith's wife ran off with the painter.
Ragwort grew on the pauper's pit.

Emmonsales Heath was the last rim of the world.
A child could see that. Once there he would kneel
And peer down over the dreadful edge of it
And learn its secrets. Just one good day's walk
Was all it needed. But night, closing in,
Found his feet tired and turning for home.

Next it was the Enclosures Man who baulked him,
Fencing the land with lines of quickthorn
And leaving him only the plod of words
To get there – words that Taylor would root up
And level out, planting crops of commas
That tore like thistles through his thoughts.

So hedged about, where else was there to go?
Safer indoors perhaps with Dr Prichard . . .
He never could have guessed they meant to chop
Off his head and steal away his alphabet,
All those pretty vowels and consonants,
Tweezering them out, one by one, through his ears.

VINCENT

he called himself,
the painter in the fields.
Vincent
he called himself,
the painter of the wind.
Vincent
he shot himself
and poppies of blood
spattered the corn.
Vincent
he shot himself
and the black rooks
flew out of his mind.

Evening, and October had hung out its damps
Down every deep and enervating lane;

But a new way to the old quarry
Blew up a fresh wind that blabbered

Into his face, loud and importunate,
Blustering spent breath back down into stuffed

Lungs again; until he turned his shoulders on it
And so found the sound gone, the great

Round sound of it quite gone,
Helpless without his ears as adversaries.

All that it was now was a whip and a whistle
Up in the hawthorn hedge and a rattle

Somewhere where it found a window loose;
At times just a high whining in the wires.

Left to itself the poor wind was nothing
But a monumental silence on the move:

An unknown poem looking for a tongue.

Between Root and Sky

'Botany . . . is a pursuit that amuses the fancy and exercises the memory, without improving the mind or advancing any real knowledge.'

Gilbert White

No, not more snow – just the petals from a windblown Blackthorn settling in the wet ruts of the lane.

LICHEN

At all frontiers;
over the tundra;
above the tree-line;
where only the granite crops,

their blue-green frost
holds hard,
subdues bare stone,
battens on sour soil.

These are the pioneers,
mapping new ground,
flourishing their shields,
their grey rosettes.

Colonisers,
preparing the way
for what is merely huge,
they move on.

TOADSTOOLS

Who
in the night
severed
all these babies'

hands
and hid them
palms uppermost
under the

walnut tree?
This morning
there are tiny
fingers

and pudgy little
nail-less thumbs
around all its
damp roots.

PIMPERNEL

Allowing into the pharmacopoeia
of the fields
only what was held
to be useful,

savants said
these scarlet sparks
among the dust and chaff
would purge a melancholy;

and picked
with all the omens so
would grant you second-sight.
But what more witch–

or leech–craft could one wish
than eyes which blink out
days that break
a little damp and drear?

LORDS AND LADIES

Blatant
in the hedge-bottom,
and poking up
like a stiff little

purple prick
that liberal shepherds
would laugh at –
a euphemism was needed:

Dead Men's Fingers,
Priest in the Pulpit.
But what's this?
Women grinding the root

to starch the courtier's ruff?
That was a new rough joke
to make the stiff-necked
yokels bleat.

HEATHER

O, Ruskin
did you really
love
the heather of Hybla

not for the hives
but the hue?
Did you keep
your distance

when you could
have had honey
dripping down your wrist
from a warm fresh crusty slice?

In *Modern Painters*
you put aside sex
as something pertaining
to spiders and flies.

LILY OF THE VALLEY

Ego sum flos campi
et lilium convallium,
said Solomon
of this ladder-to-heaven lily.

Lovers in Paris wear it
as a corsage of constancy;
and drunken in the quantitie
of a sponeful

its water restoreth speech
and does strengthen memorie;
which only makes it the more
astounding that ten minutes

after four drops were jabbed
into the veins of some poor pooch
the dumb beast lay doggo –
aye, and in Paris too.

HEMLOCK

Easeful enough
an image of it,
to safely say
'as though',

then go
for the grape instead;
but the Greek
didn't dream,

didn't break
down his door
and run;
no fears,

no fancies,
the endless
fooleries
of the body.

DANDELION

This is time's
(one o'clock, two o'clock)
golden head
wet the bed

flower;
forever turning its
(four o'clock, five o'clock)
face

to follow the sun.
But it's time that sets the
(seven o'clock, eight o'clock)
grey hairs growing

and will scythe off its
(eleven o'clock, twelve o'clock)
limp and wrinkled
ugly bald skull.

IVY

Gargoyle or saint
or blank grey wall
it is all
stone for the tendril.

Trees it chokes;
stifles
the sap's fluency.
Yet Pliny claims

a wreath of it
worn Bacchus-like
will counterpoise
the sway of wine.

Mournful
and magic plant
Horace and Virgil
took it for their crown.

FUNGUS

Spores
blowing into the dead
face of a felled birch
as it dries and splits

blossom as
orange freckles
and fine green hair;
or garish

fly agaric
blazing out of the mulch
where woodlice huddle
among crumpled ears

and shaggy parasols;
rampant in illusion,
this earth sucks
at its own insane root.

HAWTHORN

Bridewhite though it may be,
there is something
of the sweet stench
of lechery

about the hawthorn.
Mothers won't give it house-room:
unlucky – so they say.
And preachers warned

that the foulest putrefaction
of the plague pits
dwelt in its blossom –
that its smell was death.

But the brides of Beltane
still plucked it in armfuls,
wreathed it round their maypoles
and danced until they sweat.

Alonso Quixano Encounters the Sea

'I am the solitude that asks and promises nothing;
that is how I shall set you free.'

Part I

1

And he thought of Sadak, poor Herculean mite
grappling wearily with that one last overhang;
    bewildered in a mountainscape
of Martinean confectionery
    and cataracts of caramel.

2

Why Sadak though, when surely these soft sandy slopes
would lead to no such waters of oblivion?
    This gave him pause, and his nostrils
narrowed, as they sensed some new shiver
    in the damp furrows of the wind.

3

Flexing his toes he heeled off down towards the beach,
where weed and shellfish crunched and squelched beneath
            his feet:
    the flung detritus of the sea,
whose creamy, thick and overlapping foam
    glushed and spluttered along the shore

4

with an empty, high-flown fury; swaggering up
only to cringe and snivel back again; leaving
    jots on unintelligible
marginalia scribbled there in brine;
    jots which even the stalky eyes

5

of crabs which plopped and popped open like brown bubbles
in the cold silt could take no readings from; patterns
    of marbled mottling and lace.
The dumb barbaric vagueness of it all
    was what appalled Alonso most.

6

On his sea of dreams sometimes, she had held out hopes
of handsome clipper fleets flying before the trades,
    harmonious concord of keels,
with their kelsons all humming like harp-strings
    and water curdled in their wake,

7

but crewed by practical men of affairs, these all
had harbours to get to, and did not feel disposed
    to lower gigs for castaways.
So when the western horizon came rolling
    in under them, he was left

8

to founder in his sleep. Yet still Alonso sensed
that though these dwellers on the deep might scorn his strand,
    it really was the only place
where one might dabble one's dry thumbs and feel
    the rhythms of each ocean's pulse.

Part II

9

Late November it had been when he'd first set out;
not the most auspicious time of year to begin
   such a journey, when all men else,
having greased their tools against the winter,
   seemed quite content to sit and think

10

of pocky mandarins and nuts; for November
is such a quiet and downtrodden kind of month;
   it lacks the clean finality
of cold, the brittle fern-frond-on-slate
   precision of its absolute.

11

But what weighed worse, his neighbours could almost have been
the month itself, they'd such a damp and doubting air;
   their very silence lacked a voice,
was empty even of the unspoken
   resonances of those words

12

we have no need for when there's anguish near the bone.
Beset by nerves so taut a breath of wind could draw
   a chord from them, a man might well
luxuriate a while in such a peace,
   beatus ille, yet not for long;

13

the singing rocks are risky, but there's no quester
could survive their total and contemptuous mute;
   and the most myth that could be hoped
was that some kindly hand might hold an end
   while Orpheus tried to thread himself

14

through the labyrinthian eye of their nostalgia.
He knew himself climbing up out of the dark; slow
   and pensive, until his fingers
gripped the top rim of the ridge with first light.
   It was a morning neither blue

15

nor grey, the sky not a colour but a distance,
and he watched his long shadow go rippling down
   into the valley before him.
Descent was dire, but as the aggression
   of the ground grew less, knots of gorse

16

and writhen thorn gave way to quickbeam, birch and ash,
each branch as velvet as a young deer's horn, the hoarfrost
   had so textured them; and crisp grass
that squeaked underfoot as he neared his people,
   numb in their circle of sallows.

Part III

17

As once in the valley of bones Exekial,
so now he, vocable life into their marrow
    breathed, and what toppled dolmen seemed
he moved: rue-leaved or starry saxifrage
    the word that bloomed among the stone.

18

Their gloomy world of course had long before been loud
and even odorous with a brutal kind of
    statement and reply, but the word
was like warm days to frozen fields, and waked
    the faint beginnings of a tune:

19

(purple of cello under emeralds of flute)
it came with a new bloom like the patina of
    brushed plum upon it, and so took
possession of the air, life leapt with it
    and feet lifted to the measure

20

dancing the gone of winter till even the reeds
that combed at the river's edge grew melodious,
    piping with the inspiration
of the breeze eclogues of lost Arcadies.
    There were no poems, only words,

21

yet all the words that were, were poems: the concert
of myth and tongue. For it was this: the wish for things
    as they could never quite be, this
and not a thin contingency of *is*,
    that on the blue plains of Shinar

22

energised the namer, in whose lost name this dark
ivy twists once more, climbing like the winding stair
    inside a tower, where you sit
reading by lamplight in the still quiet
    of calm. Instead though, read now of

23

an ancient rowan tree high up in the mountains,
with woodsmen working to fell it. See their iron
    axes vying with stroke after
juddering stroke to bring it down. See its leaves
    shiver, and how its topmost boughs

24

begin to tremble until, vanquished at last, it
keels over with a great groan and crashes, trailing
    its havoc down the mountain's side.
Well, it was the same with your tower too,
    and with Alonso's and with mine.

25

All rummaged in the rubble's billowing smokedust
blind, snatching up what fragments of old phrases
    they could find; the fall having torn
out tongues and cut the people at their root,
    each word lost was a whole world gone,

26

while some they saved had in themselves a savour of
mortality: the greenest inference of *was*
    tasted of ashes in their mouths
and one rhyme only could be found for breath.
    So Alonso ran beside them

27

scattering all the enticements of late summer
at their feet: eglantine and marigold and musk,
    but, as deep in every flower
that they gathered, they saw time's eyelid blink,
    what use to them was his fiction?

28

If he'd woven robes of opulent silk to fling
about their shoulders, all they'd have known was the worm
    and its itch. What did they want? Poems
that told them what they knew to be true, or
    was it the truth of poetry?

29

Which, as she always said, was to see that no one
forgot what they did not know they knew: the essence
    and not the aspect; the hard seed
and not the winnowable husk. And yet
    times there are when even a seed

30

feels inside itself the pressure of its own seeds
raging to wrinkle what as yet's not ripe. Then dumb
    fear of the flail comes, men moping
at a harvest home; for after the sound
    of the deep bass-viol is done

31

and the topers have lurched off home through the darkness,
there is only the darkness; midwinter silence,
    madness or suicide: coldest
and echoic limit of all language.
    Alive, Alonso sniffed for the sea.

Part IV

32

'Like all the rest of them', she said, 'who cannot cope
with life, he took a turn with death, and when he thought
   his charm had won the day for him
he set off climbing towards the light. But
   when he stopped, as we all knew that

33

he would, and looked back over his shoulder, he found
that I was not there; but then of course I never
   had been. It is not in my nature
to be a follower. Ah, but my nails
   were soon there when my Bacchantes

34

had run him down to earth. His thin ribs we stripped out,
clawed clean and scattered among the rocks. His singing
   head we sent down Hebrus. We quelled
the rebellion of the trees, and all
   the Lesbian coves incarnadined.

35

At Tintagel I lay listening to the waves
slapping against the red-stone walls of the castle,
   and my thoughts went out like black sails
billowing towards him over the sea.
   One morning specially I recalled

36

redolent of roses in a high-walled garden;
me in a pearl-white gown of soft silk from Toulouse
    and he embroidered as the May.
It was an ordinary garden
    with the usual blemishes:

37

thorns on the roses, a thistle or a nettle
here and there; but we two might well have walked our long
    love's day together there, had he
had eyes to see things as they really were
    and not forever tried to read

38

portents and omens in particularities,
so pestering me with obtuse parallels that,
    wearied, I brought him to the brink
of these Lethean waters, and kissed him
    hard through the silence of their fall.'